DEPENDENT ORIGINATION

A TRANSLATION of the TERMS,
EXAMINATION of the LOGICAL STRUCTURE
and EXPLANATION of the MEANING

of the Buddha's Discourse

PAṬICCASAMUPPĀDA

Brian Taylor

道

UNIVERSAL OCTOPUS

Also published in Same Series:

What is Buddhism?
The Living Waters of Buddhism
Buddhism and Drugs
The Five Buddhist Precepts
Basic Buddhist Meditation
Basic Buddhism for a World in Trouble
The Ten Fetters (*Saŋyojana*)
The Five Nivāranas
(*The Buddha's Teaching of the Five Hindrances*)
Buddhist Pali Chants with English Translations

Published by Universal Octopus 2016
www.universaloctopus.com

A catalogue record of this book is available from the British
Library.

ISBN 978-0-9571901-9-1

DEPENDENT ORIGINATION

PAṬICCASAMUPPĀDA, the Buddha's Teaching of DEPENDENT ORIGINATION, is a fast-track method for experiencing Nibbāna.

It is recorded in the last book of the Abhidhamma Piṭaka. This is the third part of the Tipiṭika, the Three Baskets (Piṭaka = "baskets") of Theravadin Buddhist texts. The Abhidhamma Piṭaka is a compilation dating from after the Buddha's death. In it, various themes from the suttas are schematised in order to codify them and bring out their logical connectedness.

This booklet provides a translation of the Pali terms, an explanation of how the logical structure works and gives a comprehensive explanation of the meaning and intention.

Most Westerners find the *Dependent Origination* difficult. Consequently, when they come to translate it, they misinterpret key terms. Their attempts to explain the overall meaning are often very long and complicated, use unusual or unfamiliar words and fail to provide anything which a reader can **use**.

Easterners also find it difficult and are generally much better at memorizing and chanting it than at making clear the meaning.

And it is the **meaning** that counts. Buddhism is a practical religion. The Buddha explains how things are and what one can do to put an end to suffering forever. We are then supposed to get on and **do** something.

Until we understand the tools he supplies us with, we do not progress easily. This booklet is intended to assist this undertaking by explaining what the tools are and how to use them.

Pali is a language without its own alphabet. The Buddhist teachings, the suttas, were delivered orally by the Buddha and passed on orally by his monks for about 400 years until it was decided, at the Fourth Council, that they should be written down. No single script was ever developed for the language of the canon. Scribes used the scripts of their native languages to transcribe the texts and they have been transliterated into various languages until today.

The language Shakyamuni (the Buddha) spoke was the one in general use around the middle reaches of the Ganges, where he was active. Since the area was later called Magadha, its language was called Magadhi. Traditionally, this language has been called Pali by Theravadin Buddhists. Recently, scholars have attempted to show that Pali and

Magadhi are basically different languages. This is the kind of thing scholars do to make a living. But looking back to a period over 2500 years ago in Northern India, where there is nothing in the way of contemporary written evidence, means that there is no serious basis for their conclusions. Pali is the name which has been given to the language of the Buddha's authentic teachings. There is no reason to look any further.

For transliteration, I have mostly followed Rhys Davids and Stede in their Dictionary and Nyanatiloka and the Buddhist Publication Society.

PAṬICCASAMUPPĀDA

Avijjā-paccayā Saṅkhārā
Saṅkhāra-paccayā Viññāṇaŋ
Viññāna-paccayā Nāma-rūpaŋ
Nāma-rūpa-paccayā Saḷayatanaŋ
Saḷāyatana-paccayā Phasso
Phassa-paccayā Vedanā
Vedanā-paccayā Taṇhā
Taṇhā-paccayā Upādānaŋ
Upādāna-paccayā Bhavo
Bhava-paccayā Jāti
Jāti-paccayā Jarāmaraṇaŋ Soka
Parideva Dukkha Domanassa
Upāyāsa Sambhavanti.

DEPENDENT ORIGINATION

Avijjā forms the base for Sankhāras.
Sankhāras form the base for Consciousness.
Consciousness forms the base for Name and Form.
Name and Form form the base for the Six Sense Bases.
The Six Sense Bases form the base for Contact.
Contact forms the base for Feeling.
Feeling forms the base for Craving.
Craving forms the base for Clinging.
Clinging forms the base for Becoming.
Becoming forms the base for Birth.
Birth forms the base for Old Age, Death, Sorrow,
Lamentation, Pain, Grief and Despair.

Logical Structure

"Forms the base for" is a better way of translating **Paccayā** than "because of" or "from" and is closer to the linguistic meaning ("foundation"). "Forms the base for" indicates how the logic of this discourse works.

Imagine a column of bricks, one above the other. Each brick forms the base for the one above. This suggests that, even if the factors were to come into place one after another, once they are in place, they are all there in the present moment. Avijjā is the base brick. With Avijjā in place, all the other bricks form a column above it. Each one rests on the one below. All rest on the base brick. If you remove Avijjā, the whole column tumbles down (*see Appendix One*).

It is necessary to understand what each of the terms for each individual brick means.

1. **Avijjā** (a + vijjā). Vijjā means "**Seeing**" (cognate with "vision") and also understanding what you see (*see Appendix One*).

In this case, it means seeing the world and everything in it as it actually is, without projecting viewpoints upon what you are looking at which make it appear otherwise. This means "correct seeing" or "right view". Seeing <u>correctly</u> means seeing unsatisfactory things as unsatisfactory. **Avijjā** (a + vijjā) means <u>not</u> seeing things as they actually are. Not seeing unsatisfactory things as unsatisfactory.

2. **Sankhārā.** A Sankhāra is a **Compound**. Something made up of bits. Not a thing in itself. If you take away all the bits, there is nothing left over. Like a motor car. Apart from all the parts, put together in a certain way, there is no car. Just the <u>idea</u> of a car. Everything, mental and physical, is a Sankhāra, except Nibbāna.

If you can see everything that arises in the world and in your mind like this, then you are seeing it with Vijjā. If you see any of these Sankhāras as things in themselves, existing as separate entities rather than as part of the flow of karma (cause and effect), then you are seeing the world and the mind from the point of view of Avijjā.

Avijjā becomes the first brick. Sankhāras sit on top of it and make up the second brick. Because of false view, they appear as many <u>different</u> individual things. This makes possible the further entrapment of the mind.

3. **Viññāna.** Viññāna means **Consciousness.** Consciousness, too, cannot exist as a thing in itself.

It can only exist if there is something to be

conscious of (sense object) and an active sense organ. This threesome makes up the fundamental Sankhāra in the functioning of the human mind.

There has to be <u>something</u> to be conscious of. When a Sankhāra, mental or physical, arises and there is a sense organ to perceive it, then the presence of object and sense organ gives rise to consciousness of that object.

This is the third brick and sits on top of Sankhāras. Because Avijjā <u>is still in position</u> at the bottom of the column, consciousness appears as consciousness of <u>a separate thing in itself</u>. The mind is now one stage further in the entrapment process.

4. **Nāma-Rūpa.** Nāma-Rūpa means **Name and Form.** That is the obvious and original meaning of these words.

With your eye you see a form. But as soon as you give it a name, it makes possible a particularised interpretation of sense phenomena. You super-impose a mental concept upon the experience, upon the perceived visible object. You impose <u>viewpoint</u>:

"Is this my Ming vase or your flower pot?"

From this point on, all phenomena open the door to identification and possessiveness. Their true nature as **Anatta**, Not-Self, is hidden.

Later scholars redefined Nāma and Rūpa in terms of *mind* and *body*. A conceptual distinction was made between *mental* (feeling, perception, will, desire, consciousness etc.) and *material* (everything making up the physical universe in terms of the four elements).

This replaced the actual *experience* of the seeing of a form and labelling it. It encouraged ever more *thinking-about*. The here-and-now practical application was (and is) lost.

What Nāma and Rūpa have in common is that they are both conditioned by consciousness.

That is to say, if there were no consciousness of them, they would cease to exist for us. This doesn't mean that the world would cease to exist for us. For, as long as eyes can see and there are things to be seen, there will be and has always been consciousness of the world.

When the mind labels things, it fashions them as independently existing entities rather than seeing them as part of an impersonal causal flow.

It is like being unable to see the ocean for the waves. We end up preferring big foamy billowing rollers to tiny ripples. We give them separate names to emphasise their differentness and enshrine our points of view. We mourn their inevitable disappearance. Though we can still write their biographies. And even put our names on the title page!

Nāma-Rūpa is the fourth brick and sits on top of Consciousness. Since Avijjā is still in position at the bottom of the column, the process of entrapment proceeds.

5. **Saḷāyatana.** Saḷāyatana are the **Six Sense-Bases.** Eye, ear, nose, tongue, touch and mind. These enable sense objects to be differentiated into mental and physical and also into more particularised sense objects: sights, sounds, smells, tastes, touch. The greater the proliferation of names to fit the forms we perceive, the more discriminating mental activity becomes and the greater the detail perceived.

But since Avijjā is still in position at the bottom of the column, all the contents of this more detailed experience appear as separately existing things in themselves, rather than as an impersonal causal flow.

6. **Phassa.** Phassa is **Contact**, touch, and therefore a sense impression. Things which are flowing past are individually perceived and recorded as sense impressions (including mind impressions).

And, since Avijjā is still in position at the bottom of the column, these impressions are perceived as being separate things in themselves rather than part of the flow. One is sitting looking at the sea, and begins to see all the waves as different individuals rather than just (and only) moving water.

7. **Vedanā.** Vedanā means **Feeling**. Mental or physical. Pleasant, unpleasant or neutral.

If one is able to contemplate feeling as just feeling when it arises, without allowing it to connect with the sense object associated with it, one can stop the chain at that point. One can do this by patiently investigating feelings and seeing that all feelings have the same three characteristics:

* Impermanence
* Unsatisfactoriness
* Not-self

They are seen, therefore, as not worth grasping after. In this case, although the Vedanā brick sits squarely on the Phassa brick, seeing that all feelings are not worth grasping after prevents grasping and clinging from arising.

Effectively, one is able to introduce Vijjā, in the form of right view, at this point.

If one can't do this, then, since Avijjā <u>is still in position</u> at the bottom of the column, Vedanā becomes the base for the next brick.

8. **Taṇhā.** Taṇhā is compulsive desire. It is usually translated as **"Craving"** but really means

Thirst. If one thinks of the compulsive thirst of the alcoholic, one is not far off the meaning.

Because one experiences pleasant feelings as desirable, one desires them and becomes attached to them. The more desirable one finds them, the greater the desire.

So Taṇhā takes its place above Vedanā as the eighth brick.

Because of Avijjā, which is still in position at the bottom of the column, a cluster of characteristics in the flow of causation is seen as a thing in itself. One singles out a something which fits a point of view. The pleasant feeling it gives causes desire for that thing. This strong desire (Taṇhā) then becomes the base for the next brick.

9. **Upādāna.** Upādāna is usually translated as "clinging". Literally, it means "taking up", so **"Grasping"** might be better. The difference between Taṇhā and Upādāna is that one *craves* something which one hasn't at that moment got. Once one has it, one *clings* to it.

Again, Avijjā is still in position at the bottom of the column and makes one see the sense object as a thing in itself. One tries to grasp it and hold on to it. This is like trying to catch a wave in a fishing net and hold on to it. So grasping takes its place as the ninth brick.

10. **Bhava.** Bhava means "**Becoming**", the "flow of existence". The previous bricks create an onward flowing energy so that there is a desire and a need to become something, some independently existing, permanent entity. One thinks of oneself, under the influence of Avijjā, as a something or a someone and one wants to repeat this endlessly in the future. One wants to be forever.

Bhava rests upon Upādāna. Bhava flows into:

11. **Jāti.** Jāti means "**Birth**". The urge to become something leads to being born as that something. Even though the something itself is just a part of the flow of cause and effect. Another wave. Part of the ocean.

Once there is a Birth (a beginning) there is inevitably a Death (an ending) and, also inevitably, between Birth and Death come:

12. **Jarāmaraṇaŋ Soka Parideva Dukkha Domanassa Upāyāsa Sambhavanti.**
"Old age, death, sorrow, lamentation, pain, grief and despair."

ALL things are experienced between birth and death.

Because there are no permanent entities, columns of cause and effect rise into existence like waves in the sea, then sink down again and disappear from view. Everything, teaches the Buddha, that has a beginning has an end. Whatever is born dies. If you don't want to grow old and die, then avoid birth.

The flow of the Dependent Origination is incessant. Both in the long term, from lifetime to lifetime, and also, in the present, from moment to moment.

Escape is only possible if the Avijjā brick is removed. Then, the whole column of bricks collapses and only Vijjā remains. It is like awakening from a bad dream – a nightmare. Then, things are accepted as they are clearly seen to be, impermanent, unsatisfactory and without a self. There is no longer any desire for, or grasping after, the undesirable.

Understanding of this is not quite enough. What is needed is **seeing** the truth continuously from moment to moment. Patient investigation of all phenomena that arise in one's life results first in understanding then in seeing. If one's concentration is good and one is skilled in Buddhist meditation, the goal is reached much more quickly than if one isn't.

In either case, one's morality needs to be complete. Basic morality – Don't do to others what you don't want done to you. This normalises your relationship with your fellow beings and is a necessary prerequisite for living in peace. If one can take on board the Five Buddhist Precepts, so much the better. Basic morality helps to make the goal of Nibbāna achievable.

"If these five precepts were kept throughout the human world, it would make an unbelievable difference. There would be no war, no serious crime, and no need for money to be spent on armies, policing, courts of justice or prisons."

(from *Basic Buddhism for a World in Trouble*)

APPENDIX ONE

Avijjā:

If this term is not translated correctly and understood, the result is that open-eyed meditation on Dependent Origination cannot be practised correctly and a preview of Nibbāna, the state of Stream-Enterer, attained.

Everywhere, Avijjā is translated as "Ignorance", especially "Ignorance of the Four Noble Truths". Ignorance means not knowing.

Knowledge refers to data which is retained in the mind. It can be factually correct, "I know your aunt. I know the French for 'thank you'." It can be incorrect, "I know 2+2 = 5". In the latter case, you do know *something*; it just happens to be wrong.

Ignorance is simply *not knowing*. "I don't know your aunt. I don't know any French. I don't know 2+2 = anything."

Vijjā is usually translated as "Knowledge". But Vijjā is *different* from Knowledge. It is not just data retained in the mind. It means actually *seeing* in the present and having immediate understanding of something in the present.

Many Buddhists *know* the Four Noble Truths. They can repeat them in the way a child can repeat its nine times table. They are certainly not ignorant of them. But this knowledge is not sufficient to remove Avijja as the first step in the *Dependent Origination*. It cannot thereby bring about the psychological process which the Buddha experienced under the Bodhi tree and by which he achieved Enlightenment.

On the contrary, most Buddhists, even those who are fluent in their knowledge of the First Noble Truth, cannot even see that the food on their plates got there as the result of being bred in captivity and killed, usually painfully. They cannot see Suffering in its entirety.

So Vijjā is *not* Knowledge and Avijjā is *not* Ignorance.

Vijjā is Seeing. Seeing the First Noble Truth means seeing suffering wherever it appears, immediately and with direct, decisive understanding; the corpse on the plate, the screaming child, the widow at the funeral, the old man crying silently as he dies.

Avijjā means *not seeing* these things with immediate understanding in the present, wherever they appear.

Knowledge means just knowing things as facts, stored mentally in the memory banks together with "the sun rises in the east", "a jellyfish sting can be unpleasant", "Christmas Day celebrates the birth of Jesus, although it is believed he was born on an altogether different day". Ignorance means not even knowing the facts (i.e. not having these data in the mind).

(*See* Saŋyojana: The Buddha's Doctrine of the Ten Fetters)

APPENDIX TWO

It is important to grasp that if the Avijjā brick is removed, the whole column of bricks falls instantaneously and the problem of suffering is solved. The following true story illustrates this.

During the First World War, a middle-aged woman heard a knock on her door. When she opened it, she found an army officer in uniform.

He said he was very sorry to have to tell her that her son had been killed in action. He said that her son had been a hero who had died for his country. He asked if there was anything he could do to help her.

This had a catastrophic effect on the woman.

She had lost her only son and would have to face the future without his companionship and support. She would have to deal with all the practical consequences of his death and inform the other members of the family.

The following days brought a sense of despair and hopelessness. The meaning had gone out of her life.

Three weeks later, there was another knock on the

door. It was a different army officer in uniform. He said he had news for her. There had been a mistake. Her son had not been killed. He was alive and well.

The effect on the woman was immediate. Her grieving stopped. She lost all her concerns about facing a future alone and without her son. There were now no practical consequences of his death that she would have to deal with.

Five minutes before, she had been in despair. Now she was happy and relieved.

But her son had not come back from the dead. Nothing in the outside world had actually changed. He had been alive all along. It was just that the contents of her mind had changed. Instantaneously.

Or consider an old bucket that has stood for a long time in the garden, filling to the brim with rain and debris. One day the gardener lifts it and the rusted bottom falls out. Everything that rested on the bottom, *irrespective of what it is,* falls out instantly.

So it is with the Avijjā brick. Once it is removed. The column, with all the other bricks, collapses. In the present. Freedom from suffering and Nibbāna are attained.

APPENDIX THREE

Dependent Origination should not be considered as either a scholastic or etymological treatise. It is a practical psychological explanation of how suffering arises and the psychological steps to be taken in the here and now to reach enlightenment directly.

It is the Buddhist equivalent of the account of The Fall of Man recorded in the Book of Genesis.

But unlike Genesis it provides a way of *reversing* The Fall. The Jews had to wait until the coming of the Messiah for a practical instruction for re-entering the Garden of Eden or The Kingdom of Heaven.

www.ingramcontent.com/pod-product-compliance
Lightning Source LLC
Chambersburg PA
CBHW020449030426

42337CB00014B/1475